Scratch Beginner Lesson Book

Anugraha K. G.

About me

Hi, I'm a student who loves coding. I'm excited to be publishing my very first book, all about Scratch!

The very first time I tried coding, it was on Scratch — and I was instantly drawn in ! I loved how creative and fun it is. Scratch isn't just about writing code. It's like telling a story or building a game with your brain. That's what makes it so interesting to me and curious to know more.

This is why I wrote this book to help young minds like you explore and discover how awesome Scratch can be.

I hope this book helps you learn and create with confidence.

Thanks for joining me on this coding adventure!

YOU'VE GOT THIS!!

TABLE OF CONTENTS

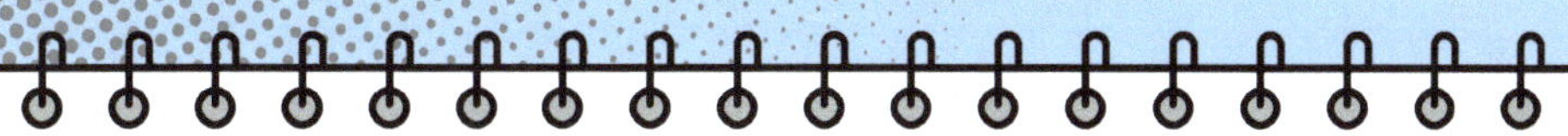

C1: Getting Started

By the end of this chapter, you should be able to:
- Understand what Scratch is and why it's useful.
- Identify key components of the Scratch page.
- Create and save a simple Scratch project.
- Move a sprite using basic blocks.

What is scratch?

https://scratch.mit.edu

Visual programming language developed by MIT that allows users to create interactive stories, animations, and games using drag-and-drop coding blocks.

Creating an account

If you don't have a scratch account, the projects you make won't be stored

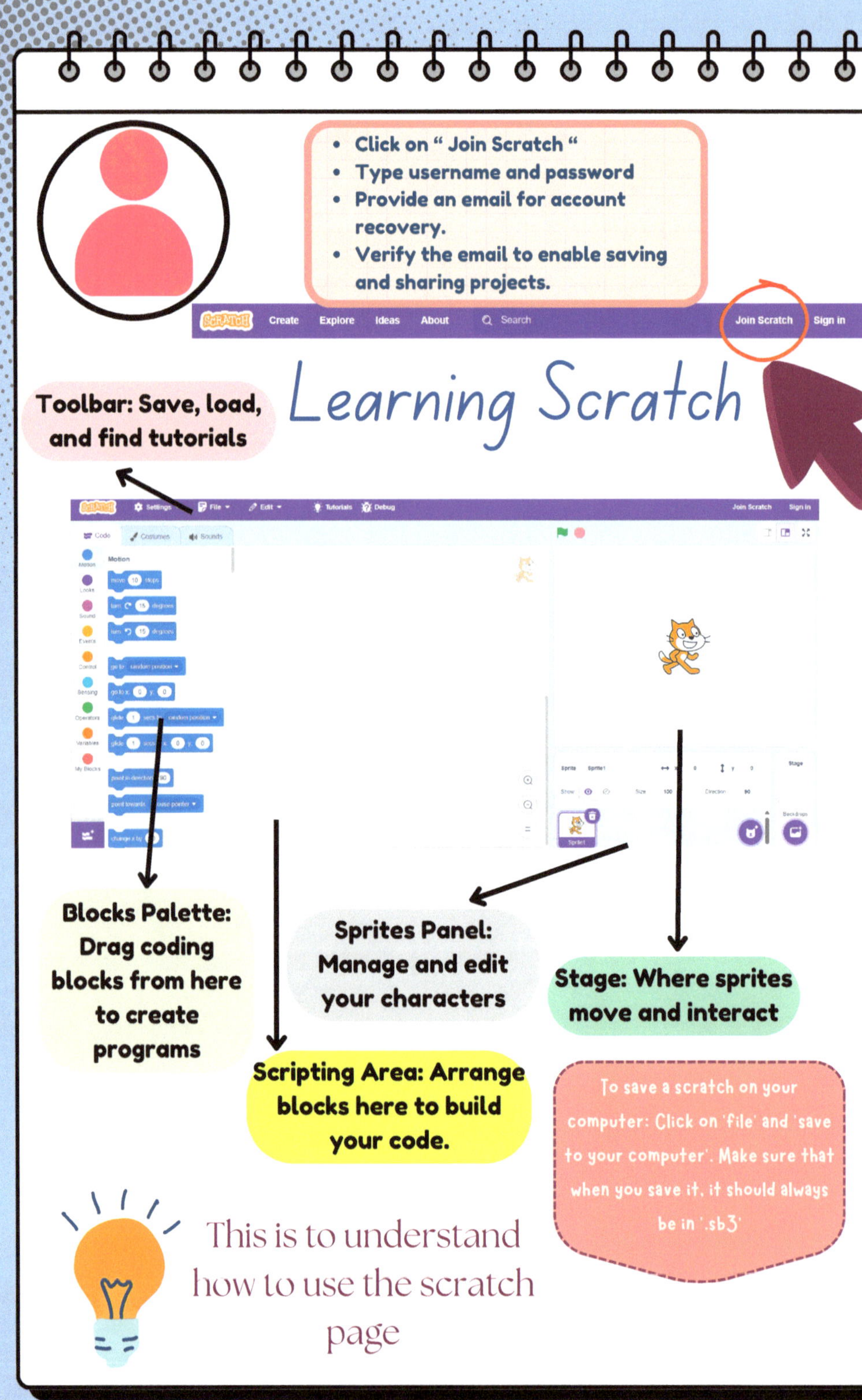

Click on " Join Scratch "
Type username and password
Provide an email for account recovery.
Verify the email to enable saving and sharing projects.

Create   Explore   Ideas   About   Search   Join Scratch   Sign in

Toolbar: Save, load, and find tutorials

Learning Scratch

Settings   File   Edit   Tutorials   Debug   Join Scratch   Sign in
Code   Costumes   Sounds
Motion

Blocks Palette: Drag coding blocks from here to create programs

Sprites Panel: Manage and edit your characters

Stage: Where sprites move and interact

Scripting Area: Arrange blocks here to build your code.

To save a scratch on your computer: Click on 'file' and 'save to your computer'. Make sure that when you save it, it should always be in '.sb3'

This is to understand how to use the scratch page

First Project

1. Selecting a Sprite

- Every Scratch project starts with a sprite (default is the Scratch Cat).
- Keep the default Scratch Cat.
- Choose a new sprite by clicking the "Choose a Sprite" button.

2. Making the Sprite Move

- Introduce basic Motion Blocks:
  - Drag the "when green flag clicked" block (found in Events).
  - Attach the "move 10 steps" block (found in Motion).
  - Click the green flag to test.

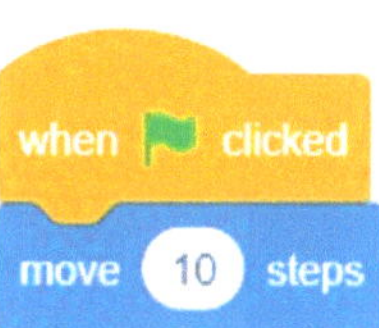

3. Adding User Control

- Try the "when key pressed" block (Events).
- Connect the "move 10 steps" block to allow movement when the right arrow key is pressed.
- Add another script for the left arrow key (using "move -10 steps").

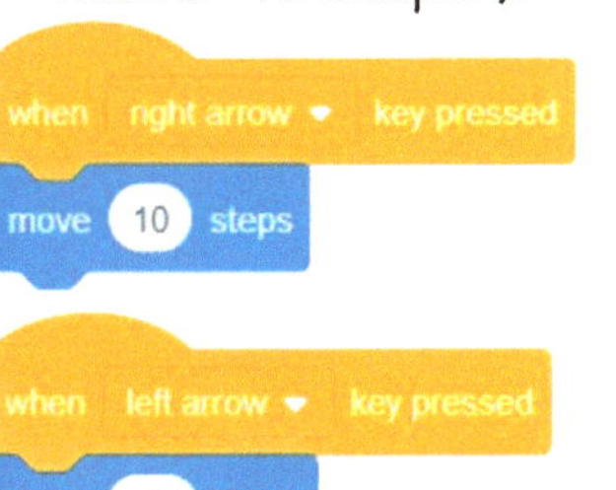

Challenge: Try making the sprite to move up and down as well

START

FINAL TASK: Create a scratch project which can allow a sprite(does not have to be a cat) to move around when a key is pressed. Try to add a background by exploring the options on the bottom left.

C2: Scratch Blocks

By the end of this chapter, you should be able to:
- Identify the different types of Scratch blocks.
- Use Events and Motion blocks to create simple interactions.
- Create a basic interactive animation using Looks and Sound blocks.

TYPES OF SCRATCH BLOCKS

Motion — Controls the movement of sprites.

Looks — Changes how sprites appear and talk

Sound — Adds sound effects or music.

Events — Start actions when something happens

Control — Repeat or control actions using loops and conditions.

Sensing — Detect user input (keyboard, mouse, sprite contact).

Operators — Perform math and logic operations.

Variables — Store and change values like scores and timers.

My Blocks — Custom blocks that you create for specific tasks.

Tip: Blocks are found in the Blocks Palette on the left side of the Scratch editor.

Creating an interactive animation

Step 1: Choose a Sprite

- Click the **Choose a Sprite** button and **pick a character.**

Step 2: Add Motion and Looks

- Drag **"when green flag clicked"** from Events.
- Attach **"move 10 steps"** from Motion.
- Add **"Say Hello! for 2 seconds"** from Looks.

Step 3: Add a Loop

- Attach a **"forever"** block from Control.
- Add **"move 10 steps"** inside the forever block.

Test what happens!

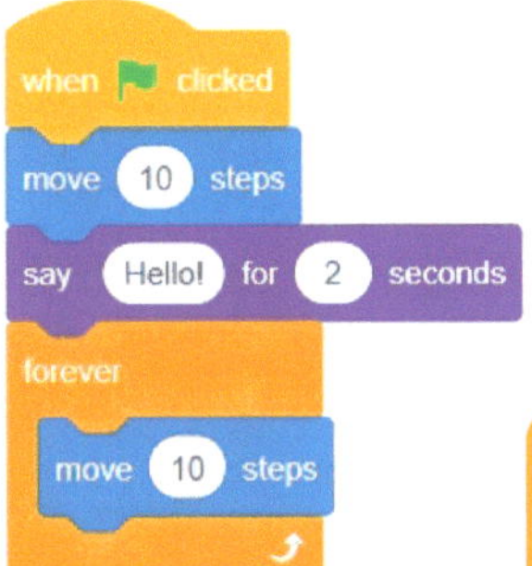

Fixing Errors

ERROR 1: FORGETTING TO CONNECT BLOCKS.
SOLUTION: MAKE SURE ALL BLOCKS SNAP TOGETHER.
ERROR 2: SPRITES MOVING TOO FAST.
SOLUTION: ADD A "WAIT 1 SECOND" BLOCK TO SLOW DOWN ACTIONS.

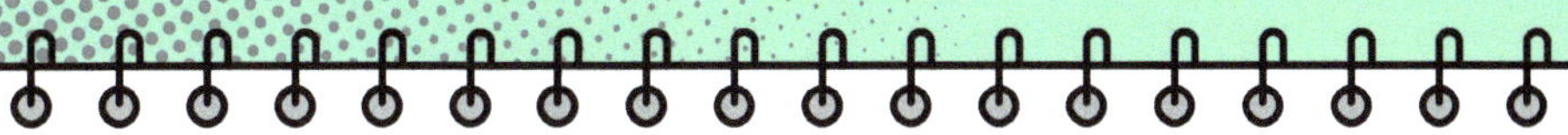

C3: Control and Sensing

By the end of this chapter, you should be able to:
- Use loops to repeat actions and conditionals to make decisions.
- Detect user input (mouse, keyboard) and sprite interactions.
- Create a program where a sprite reacts based on its surroundings.

Control Blocks:
- Forever Loop
- Repeat Loop
- Repeat Until Loop
- IF / THEN
- IF / ELSE
- Wait until

Sensing Blocks:
- Touching
- Key pressed
- Mouse Down
- Loudness
- Ask and wait

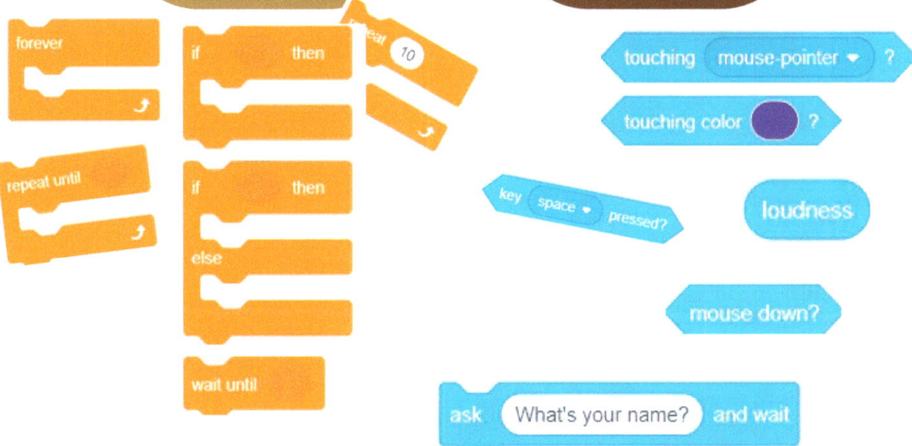

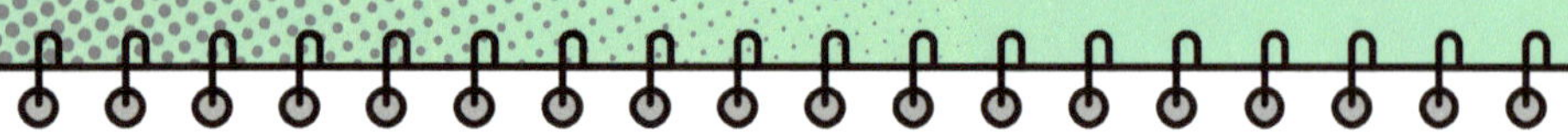

Creating an Interactive Reaction Game

Step 1: Moving the Cat with the Keyboard

- Drag "when green flag clicked" from the Events category.
- Attach a forever block from the Control category.
- Inside the loop, add "if key (space) pressed?" from the Sensing category.
- Inside the "if" block, add "move 10 steps" from the Motion category.

Step 2: Making the Ball React When Touched

- Click Choose a Sprite and select a Ball sprite.
- Drag "when green flag clicked" from the Events category.
- Attach a forever block from the Control category.
- Inside, add "if touching Cat(SPRITE 1) ?" from the Sensing category.
- Inside the "if" block, add "say Ouch! for 2 seconds" from the Looks category.

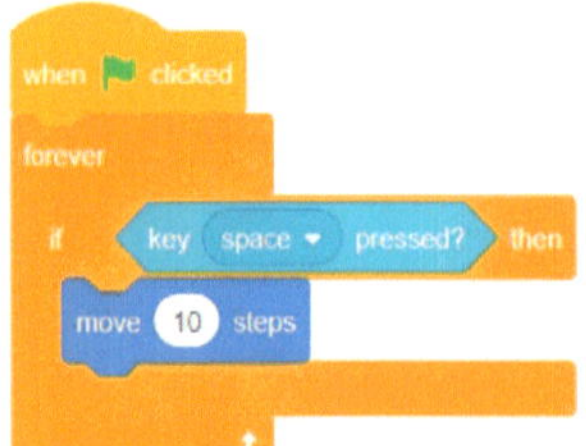

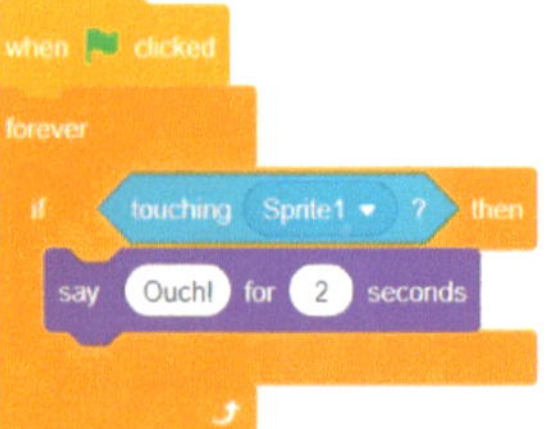

Challenge: Enhance this code by making the cat move in 4 directions and the ball has to keep moving.

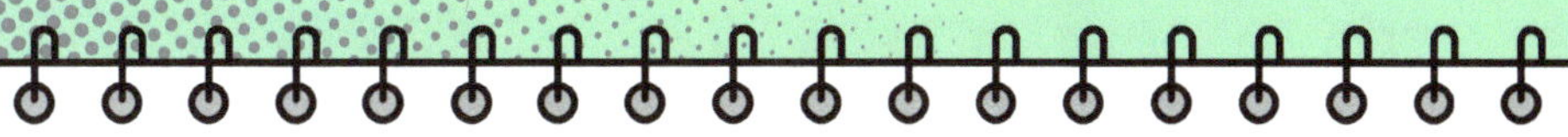

COMMON MISTAKES

- Problem: The sprite keeps moving without pressing the key.
  - Solution: Check that the "if key pressed" block is inside a forever loop.
- Problem: The sprite does not react when touched.
  - Solution: Make sure the "touching mouse-pointer?" block is used inside a loop.

C4: Variables and Functions

By the end of this chapter, you should be able to:
- Use variables to store and change data.
- Create a score system for a game.
- Understand functions (custom blocks) to make code more efficient.

Variable: store numbers or text, and they can change while the program runs.
Where to Find Variables in Scratch?
- Click the Variables category in the Blocks Panel.
- Click "Make a Variable" and give it a name.
- Choose whether the variable should be for all sprites or for this sprite only.

Eg:
1. Go to Variables and click "Make a Variable". Name it Score.
2. Drag "when green flag clicked" from Events.
3. Add "set Score to 0" from Variables.
4. Select the Ball sprite.
5. Drag "if touching Cat?" from Sensing.
6. Inside, add "change Score by 1" from Variables.

A function (custom block) is a set of instructions that can be reused multiple times. This helps to keep the code organized and avoid repetition.
Creating a Custom Function
1. Click the My Blocks category.
2. Click "Make a Block" and name it Move and Bounce.
3. Click OK to create the function.

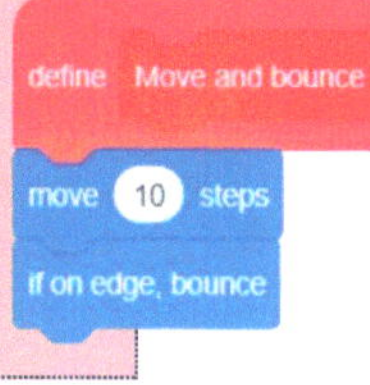

A GAME

1. Set Up the Ball's Code
1. **When Green Flag Clicked**
   - **Set Score to 0 (to reset at the start).**
   - **Run the game in a forever loop.**
2. **If the Ball touches the Cat**
   - **Increase Score by 1.**
   - **Hide the Ball.**
   - **Wait 0.5 seconds.**
   - **Move to a random position.**
   - **Show the Ball again.**

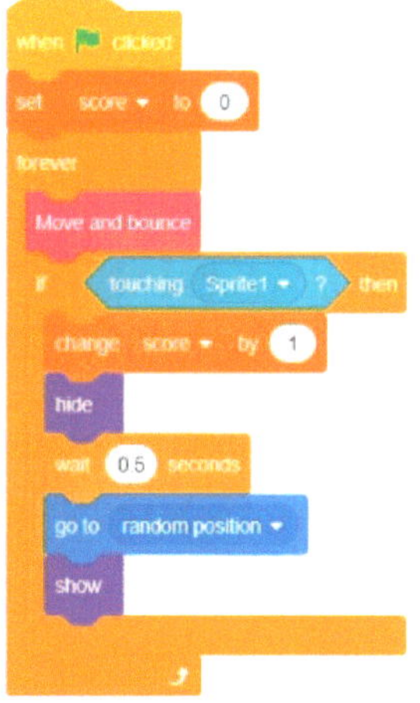

2. Move and Bounce Function for Cat
The Cat sprite should move around the screen so reuse the code from the previous part when we talked about the making a block

C5: Tips and Tricks

Best Practices for Scratch Projects

1. Organize Your Code
   - Use comments for clarity.
   - Group related blocks and create custom blocks.

2. Naming Sprites and Variables
   - Use descriptive names (e.g., "Player" instead of "Sprite1").

3. Use Broadcast Messages
   - Replace multiple forever loops with broadcasts (e.g., "Game Over").

2. Debugging Your Scratch Projects
2.1 Common Errors and Fixes
- Sprite not moving? Check if it's hidden or blocked by another sprite.
- Loops not stopping? Use "wait until" blocks to control conditions properly.
- Variables not updating? Ensure you are using "change by" instead of "set to" when needed.
2.2 Using the "Say" Block for Testing
- Use the say [message] for [x] seconds block to display variable values while testing.
- Example: If your score isn't increasing, make the sprite say the current score to check if it updates.

3. Enhancing Animations and Interactions
3.1 Smoother Movements
- Use glide instead of "go to" for smoother sprite movement.
- Example: glide (1) secs to x:(100) y:(100).
3.2 Adding Randomness
- Use pick random for unpredictability.
  - - Example: go to x: (pick random -100 to 100) y: (pick random -100 to 100).

C6: FINAL PROJECT

1.1 Project Requirements

Your quiz game must:

- **Include** at least five questions on a topic of your choice.
- **Utilise** loops, conditionals, and variables to track the player's progress.
- **Implement** sensing or broadcast messages to manage interactions.
- **Have a scoring system** that updates based on correct or incorrect answers.
- **Include** sound and visual effects to enhance the experience.
- **Display** a final score screen at the end of the quiz.
- **Test and debug your work!**

2. Planning Your Quiz Game

Before you start coding, consider:

- **What topic will your quiz cover?**
- **How will the player provide answers (typing, multiple choice, etc.)?**
- **How will you give feedback on correct or incorrect answers?**
- **What occurs when the quiz ends?**

3. Implementing Your Quiz Game

- **Create a sprite** to display questions and track answers.
- **Use variables** to store the player's score.
- **Add broadcast messages** to transition between questions.
- **Implement a timer** or limited attempts for added challenge.

* 9 7 9 8 8 9 9 0 6 5 2 1 7 *